rag rugs

rag rugs

15 step-by-step projects for hand-crafted rugs

Consultant Editor: Juju Vail

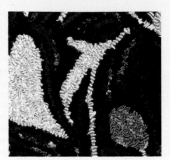

First published in 2002 by
New Holland Publishers (UK) Ltd
www.newhollandpublishers.com
London • Cape Town • Sydney • Auckland

Garfield House
86–88 Edgware Road
London W2 2EA

80 McKenzie Street
Cape Town 8001
South Africa

Level 1, Unit 4, 14 Aquatic Drive
Frenchs Forest, NSW 2086
Australia

218 Lake Road
Northcote, Auckland
New Zealand

10 9 8 7 6 5 4 3 2 1

ISBN 1 85974 879 1

Senior Editor: Clare Hubbard
Editor: Krystyna Mayer
Design: Fiona Roberts at Design Revolution Ltd
Photographer: Shona Wood
Production: Hazel Kirkman
Editorial Direction: Rosemary Wilkinson

Reproduction by Modern Age Repro House Ltd, Hong Kong
Printed and bound in Malaysia by Times Offset (M) Sdn. Bhd.

DISCLAIMER
The information in this book has been carefully researched and all efforts have been made to ensure accuracy.
The author and publisher asume no responsibility for any injuries, damages or losses incurred either during,
or subsequent to, following the instructions in this book.

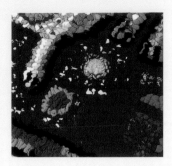

Contents

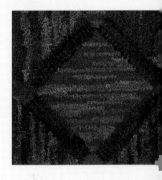

Projects

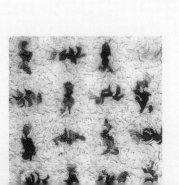

INTRODUCTION

The rug is one of the first things we look at when we come into a room. It plays a pivotal role in any decoration scheme and its colour, pattern and texture can be used to set design themes. Its shape can also influence the way you use a room, designating different areas and directing the flow of traffic. Yet it is difficult to find exactly the shape, colour, size and pattern that will provide the kind of impact that you desire without having a rug custom made at an exorbitant price. By making a rug yourself, you can have control over all the design elements. Moreover, if you make your rug out of rags, it will cost you hardly anything at all.

Rag-rug making is a traditional craft. In Britain and North America the techniques that were most commonly used were hooking, prodding, braiding and weaving. These methods are now enjoying a revival, inspired partly by the desire to transform recycled materials into unique, hand-crafted pieces for the home.

There is much speculation about whether the technique of hooking and prodding rags through hessian began in Britain and was brought to North America by settlers, or whether it originated in North America. Hessian was first imported to Britain and North America in around 1850, and the oldest surviving examples of hooked rag rugs, dating from about this time, come from the eastern United States and from Quebec and the Maritime Provinces of Canada. Earlier examples have, however, been found in North America; in these rugs, linen with some of its warp and weft threads removed was used in place of hessian.

Many wonderful examples of old rag rugs have survived, particularly in North America, where the craft was very popular. Made from old feed sacks, they usually measured about 80 x 110cm (31½ x 43½in). A house would typically have some rugs with utilitarian designs that would be used every day and some that were reserved for the parlour or for special guests. For everyday use, designs of swirling lines made up of odd ends of rags were very common in what were called Mish-mash rugs. Checks and other geometric designs were also popular because they could be drawn on to the hessian without making special templates. These rugs often seem sympathetic to modern interiors.

Many of the treasured rugs that were reserved for special occasions have survived because they were kept away from household traffic. There is a great deal of variation in their designs. Printed designs of flowers, animals and boats were often employed; no two of these designs looked exactly the same because the rags used always varied. Other designs were inspired by the imagination of their makers and included combinations of geometric and animal shapes, slogans, people, houses and many other scenes.

Rag rugs have an enduring appeal. The techniques for making them are easily mastered and the abundance of materials that can be used for them is readily and inexpensively available. The techniques used in this book include hooking, prodding (clipping) and braiding. They require very little equipment and in no more than a couple of hours you will be working at speed.

The most common rag rug is a hooked rug, which has small loops of rag that have been drawn up through a hessian background. The pile is usually short and the design is clear to see. A prodded or clipped rug (they look the same, but a slightly different technique is used to achieve them) has a shaggy rag pile. A braided rug is made of braids of rag fabric that have been joined together.

The opening chapter explains the general techniques. You can use these to design and make your own rug, unique to your particular setting, or you can follow one of the project patterns designed for contemporary interiors. Of course, the rags that you find will inspire your own personal variations, ensuring that your rug is unique.

MATERIALS

Much of the pleasure of making rag rugs comes from finding the materials. Fabrics that look unattractive in an old item of clothing are transformed when included in a rag rug. Rag materials are widely available and inexpensive, but it is impossible to predict what you will find; this is what makes each rug unique. Old clothes, household textiles and wrappings are all good sources. Fabrics that you can use include sweaters (particularly old shrunken ones in which the wool has felted), blankets, curtains, towels, nets, yarns, twisted newspaper, plastic bags, fur, feathers, candy wrappers, dresses, jackets, coats, T-shirts and socks.

While any material can be used in a rag rug, certain fabrics will make it easier to carry out the technique. Hooked rugs are easiest to make if the rag material has a lot of give and some loft; thus knitted fabrics are much easier to work than stiff, heavy fabrics. The best materials include T-shirts, wool sweaters, synthetic knits, lightweight cottons, nets and plastic bags. Heavy woven wools may also be suitable, but the rag strips need to be narrower. Very heavy, stiff fabrics like new denim are difficult to hook and are more suitable for prodded rugs, where a firm fabric is preferable. When making a braided rug avoid fabrics that fray easily and when selecting materials, bear in mind that the pattern on a fabric will be visible.

Top: balls of rags; *above:* rug canvas and hessian.

QUANTITY OF RAG FABRIC

The amount of fabric needed to make a rug depends on the technique to be used, the thickness of the fabric and the length and density of the pile (if there is one). It is best to collect a wide variety of fabrics in your chosen colours, say a large bag full and to add more fabric if you need it as you work. If you are hooking or prodding a rug, you can work out a rough estimate of how much fabric you will need by cutting a 50 x 50cm (20 x 20in) piece of fabric that is typical of the type of fabric that you intend to use. Work the fabric square, then measure the worked patch and divide the size of the finished rug by the size of this patch. Multiply this number by 40 to arrive at the number of square centimetres of fabric you will need.

If you are using one particular fabric in a large area, you may find it difficult to obtain enough fabric from a single second-hand garment. You could buy either new material or several fabrics or garments of a similar colour and blend them together. You could also dye new or old fabric with a commercial dye.

BASE FABRIC

Hooked and prodded rugs require a base fabric to hold the rug pile. Traditionally the base fabric has always been hessian, which comes in different weights or thread counts and different colours. The most common weights are 8, 10 and 12 ounces. The weight corresponds to the thread count number (sometimes called the epi) which is the number of warp threads per inch. The higher the thread count (usually the lighter the weight) the denser the fabric will be. An 8-ounce hessian might have 10 warp threads per inch and would be most suitable for a finely hooked rug, while a 12-ounce hessian has a loose weave and will be the easiest to use with a spring clip tool, where you need some room to manoeuvre the tool. A 10-ounce hessian is the most versatile and commonly used weight of base fabric. Hessian is available in either a natural beige colour or dyed in a variety of colours. In most cases you will not see the base so the colour is unimportant.

Although all the hooked, prodded and clipped rugs in this book could be made using hessian as a base fabric, some makers have used rug canvas, particularly for the prodded and clipped rugs. Rug canvas is not the same as painting or sailing canvas. It is a stiff fabric with enlarged holes between warp and weft threads. You do not need to use a frame to make a rug with rug canvas, but the rug will need a coating of adhesive on the back to hold the rag strips in place.

BACKING FABRIC

When completed, rugs may be backed either with hessian or with printed, dyed or plain cotton fabrics. You can also use twill tape in a suitable colour to edge the circumference of the backing.

TOOLS & EQUIPMENT

Rag-rug making requires very little equipment and none that is expensive. It may, however, not be readily available; rag-rug hooks and prodding tools are not usually sold in craft stores and may need to be ordered from a specialist supplier (see pages 78–79).

The tools and equipment needed depend on which rag-rug technique you are using – braided rugs require little more than a needle, while a hooked rug requires a hook, frame and scissors. In this book, the specific equipment needed is listed with each project. The various tools that can be used for each technique are described below, as is the equipment that is common to all the techniques.

The one item that is essential to all techniques is a good pair of *heavy scissors*. You may also want to use a *cutting mat* and a *rotary cutter* for cutting the rag strips. This makes the job of cutting many strips of fabric much faster and easier on the hands than if you were using scissors. A *tape measure* is useful, as is a *yardstick*, for drawing the rug dimensions and pattern grids on to the hessian. *Pins*, *safety pins*, *needle* and *thread* are useful for stitching linings to rugs.

HOOKED & PRODDED RUGS

To start with, you will need a thick *permanent marker* for drawing the rug design on to the hessian. If you do a lot of rug making and like to make detailed designs, you may want to invest in a *projector*, which can be used to enlarge the paper design to the size of the rug.

Traditionally hooked and prodded rugs are made with hessian on a *frame*. A 50 x 50cm (20 x 20in) canvas stretcher frame, available from art-supply shops, is a good frame to start with because it makes a rug portable and easy to remount as the hessian goes slack. You will need a *staple gun* suitable for wood to mount the hessian on to the

canvas stretcher frame and a *staple remover*. If you want to work on a number of projects, you may find it worthwhile to invest in a purpose-built rug frame. This is available from mail-order suppliers (see pages 78–79).

A canvas stretcher can be used as a frame for hooking by resting most of the frame on a table, but for larger frames and prodded rugs you will need to support the frame on a pair of waist-high *trestles*. These will need to be secured with *G-clamps*.

To make a hooked rug you need a *hook*. A rag-rug hook has a short, rounded handle with a crochet-type hook on the end. The handle fits into the palm of your hand. (If you were to use a crochet hook, the end would jab your palm uncomfortably.) A hook with a latch is also unsuitable. Rug hooks generally come in two sizes: primitive and extra-fine. Primitive hooks are commonly used for hooking with rags. A fine hook is more suitable for wool yarns and very finely cut wool flannel. These hooks can be purchased through mail-order suppliers (see pages 78-79).

Prodding tools are used for making prodded rugs. Anything that can poke rag strips through the hessian can be used: a knitting needle or a bradawl are adequate, but purpose-made wooden and steel prodding tools are easier to use and can be bought through mail-order suppliers. You can also use a *spring clip tool* to achieve the same look with a slightly different technique. Unlike prodded rugs, clippies are worked with the right side facing the maker.

You may want to coat the back of a prodded or hooked rug with a *latex adhesive* to improve its durability and make it less slippery. Latex adhesives are sold in hardware stores for gluing carpet tiles to the floor. An old credit card or piece of heavy card is perfect for spreading the latex over the backing.

Selection of hooking and prodding tools.

SPECIAL NOTE

The techniques described in this section follow the traditional, conventional way of making rugs and can be used to make any of the projects in this book. However, makers do develop their own individual techniques and this is reflected in the instructions to the projects. Sometimes these techniques achieve a slightly different look, or it is purely because the maker finds them easier to execute. In time you will probably develop your own techniques, which will be a hybrid of traditional methods and your own personal approach. This flexibility is the joy of making rag rugs.

1 – yardstick
2 – pins
3 – frame
4 – latex adhesive

5 – tape measure
6 – cutting mat
7 – heavy scissors
8 – needles and thread

9 – staple remover
10 – spring clip tool
11 – prodding tool
12 – hook

13 – permanent markers
14 – rotary cutter
15 – staple gun

TRANSFERRING THE RUG DESIGN

To make the hooked, prodded and clipped rugs in this book you will need to transfer the designs on to hessian or rug canvas. You may like to draw them freehand, which will be the easiest method for the simple geometric designs. Use two different coloured markers so that you can make corrections. Start by drawing the design with a jumbo red marker, then stand back and look at the design. Make corrections with a bold black marker, then trace over the entire design with the black marker.

Often the easiest way to transfer a design is to make templates of the main motifs. Motifs can be enlarged on a photocopier, then cut out and reassembled (if they are larger than the paper) and pinned to the hessian. Stand back and look at the design. When you are happy with the placement,

trace around the motifs with a marker pen, using a different colour marker for any corrections (1).

If the rug design is more complicated or as a beginner you are slightly hesitant, you will need to scale the design up on a grid (or with a projector). To scale a design on to hessian using a grid, place a grid drawn on acetate on top of the design (2). With a marker, draw a grid on to the hessian that bears the same ratio to the acetate grid as the finished rug does to the design (3). Following the grid, copy the design on to the hessian with a marker pen, using a different colour marker to correct any mistakes (4).

When positioning the design on to the hessian or canvas, allow a margin of at least 15cm (6in) around the outside of the rug for a hem and for stapling to the stretcher frame.

PREPARING RAGS

If you are using second-hand clothes and materials for rug making, it is a good idea to give them a machine wash on a hot cycle, then tumble dry them. (Wool items may felt during this process, which will actually make them even better to work with.) Fabric softener will help to make the rags more workable. New materials should also be cleaned to remove finishes.

To make the preparation of rag strips for hooking and prodding easier, remove the seams, buttons, zips and other notions from garments (1, 2 and 3). If you have a rotary cutter, it is very easy to cut the material into strips of roughly equal width (4). If you are using scissors, you may want to fold the garment pieces so that you can cut through more than one layer at a time (5). The width of the strips will depend on which technique you choose, as well as on the material and your preference. As a rough guide, try using strips about 2cm (1in) wide of a medium-weight T-shirt material, or 1cm (½in) wide of a lightweight wool sweater. Experiment to find your own preferences. Sort the rags into different colour groups and store them in clear plastic bags, so that you can find the appropriate fabrics easily.

If you like the look of aged rugs, you may want to immerse the rag fabrics in tea, coffee or onion baths to mellow their colours.

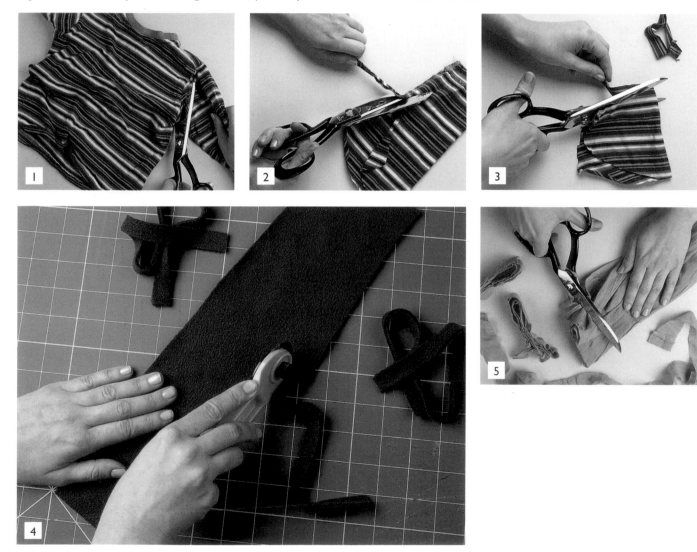

USING A STRETCHER FRAME

Most hooked and prodded rugs are made on a frame to keep the hessian taut. However, rugs worked on rug canvas do not need to be mounted on a frame to keep the base fabric taut, as it is already very stiff. Some people hook hessian-backed rugs without a frame since this makes their work more portable; but this can make the hooking slower and cause discomfort in the back and shoulders. If you use a small canvas stretcher frame the rug will be portable enough to move around. An embroidery hoop is not suitable because it is not strong enough.

The rug frame will probably be much smaller than the size of the rug. It is usually best to start hooking or prodding in the middle and move the frame around as you need to; the hessian will become increasingly less taut as you work and will need restretching anyway.

If you buy a frame especially designed for rug-making, the manufacturer's instructions will best describe how to attach the hessian, but if you want to make your own frame, buy a set of canvas stretchers and make a frame of about 50 x 50cm (20 x 20in) (1). Begin by laying the hessian flat on the floor and positioning the frame on top. Fold the hessian over the frame along one side and staple at one corner, then staple the fabric at the centre and second corner of the frame. Add more staples at 2cm (1in) intervals between the three staples. Pulling the fabric as taut as possible, stretch the hessian over the opposite edge of the frame. Fold it back over the edge and staple it at the centre of this side (2). Then moving 2cm (1in) to the right of the centre staple, again pull the fabric as taut as possible and staple. Move to the left of the centre staple and repeat this process, stapling at 2cm (1in) intervals and finishing with a staple in each corner. Continue like this along the other sides of the frame, pulling the fabric taut as you work.

Once you have completed a section of the rug, you will need to pull out the staples with the staple remover and repeat the process. You may have to staple the rug through the pile. Pull the pile aside so that you are stapling only the hessian to the frame.

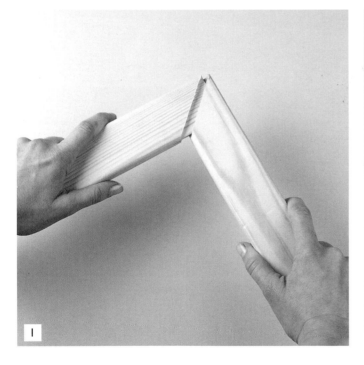

HOOKING

The rag strips in a hooked rug are not held in place by any kind of knot. They stay securely in the rug because the warp and weft threads of the hessian become displaced by the rag thickness and squeeze the pile in place.

Once you have stretched the hessian on to a frame and prepared some rag materials, sit comfortably at a table with the main part of the frame balancing on the table and part of it extending off the table, so that you can position one hand under the frame. Alternatively, support all four corners of the frame on trestles, using G-clamps. The rug should be about half-way between your waist and chest when you are seated.

'Sardines' on pages 45–47 is made using the hooking technique.

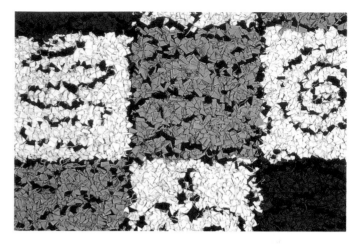

2 Poke the hook through the weave of the hessian and grab the strip with the hook. This photograph shows what is happening on the underside of the rug.

1 Hooked rugs are made with the right side facing you. Use your writing hand to hold the hook above the hessian. Beneath the hessian, use the thumb and forefinger of your other hand to hold the cut strip, ready to guide it into the hook. The arm under the hessian should be bent at the elbow. If you are stretching into the middle of the frame, you may get a backache, so try to maintain good posture as you work. Move the hessian to a different position on the frame to avoid stretching.

3 Pull the end of the strip up through the weave to the top of the rug, being careful not to grab any of the hessian in the hook, so that you have a tail of at least 1cm (½in).

4 Now poke the hook back down into a different gap in the warp and weft that is next to (or near) the rag end and pull a loop to the top of the hessian. A loop of between 0.5cm (¼in) and 1cm (½in) is standard for most 'primitive-style' hooking, but you can experiment with this to achieve a look you like. Repeat the process by poking the hook near the last loop and drawing up another loop.

5 When ending the row of hooking, pull the remainder of the strip through to the right side. Trim the ends of the strip to match the rest of the pile height. You may need to practise for 30 minutes or so before you can avoid pulling the hessian threads along with the strip, but you should be able to work quite quickly once you have mastered this step.

6 Make sure that you hook a pile dense enough to displace the threads in the weave of the hessian, otherwise the rag strips will pull out easily. However, the pile may be too densely hooked if it becomes hard to pull the rag loops up. Continue hooking until the hessian surface is covered. You can choose to hook in parallel lines, concentric circles or outline your motifs.

7 You may prefer to shear off all the loops. This will give you a smoother, denser looking pile. To do this, wait until you have completed a few centimetres, then press the pile upwards with your hand below the hessian and clip the pile with a strong pair of scissors.

PRODDING

Prodded rugs have a long, shaggy pile, which is achieved by poking rag strips down through a hessian ground fabric. For this reason, they are worked with the underside of the rug facing you. If you are using hessian fabric it must be stretched taut on a frame as explained on page 14. Prodded rugs are easiest to work if the frame is clamped to trestles, but they may also be worked with most of the frame resting on a table. To prepare the rags for prodding, cut a number of fabric strips measuring about 2 x 9cm (1 x 3½in).

Perfect your prodding technique by making the Lavender Field rug on pages 27–29.

1 Working with the underside of the rug facing you, use the prodding tool to force a small hole in between the weave of the hessian.

2 Push through one end of a strip of rag fabric.

3 Move along about 0.5cm (¼in) and make another opening in the weave of the hessian. Push through the other end of the rag strip.

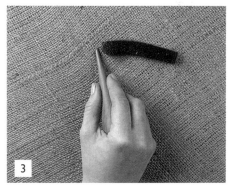

4 With the hand that is not holding the prodding tool, guide the rag strip through under the hessian, pulling the ends of the strip until they are even in length. This photograph shows the right side of the rug at this stage.

5 Prod a second strip of fabric through the rug in the same way about 0.5cm (¼in) from the last one. Continue prodding until the surface of the rug is covered and no hessian can be seen on the right side of the rug.

6 When the prodding is complete, check that the pile is even and trim any long ends if necessary.

CLIPPING

A clippy rug looks the same as a prodded rug but is made using a different tool. Stretch the hessian on a frame and prepare the rags in the same way as for prodded rugs. Work a clippy with the right side facing you and both hands above the surface.

This colourful Shaggy Rug, shown on pages 48–50, is made using the clipping technique.

1 With the clip closed, push the tool down through the weave of the hessian and then up about 0.5cm (¼in) away.

2 Open the clip and grab one end of the rag strip.

3 Hold the other end of the rag in your free hand, then pull the clip back through the hessian. Adjust the ends of the rag so that they are equal.

4 Continue in this manner until the surface of the rug is covered and no hessian can be seen on the right side of the rug.

5 Trim any pile that is uneven.

BRAIDING

Sewing braided rags together is a traditional way of creating a rag rug. This can be done in many different ways. The most common design is a coiled braid, forming a circular or oval shape. Other shapes can be made by creating clusters of small, coiled braids, which are then edged with a braid. Shorter pieces can lie next to each other to make rectangular rugs.

The width of braiding strips can vary depending on the type of fabric you use and how chunky you want the rug to be. It is best to choose fabrics that are of a similar weight, keeping fabrics of dress weights for one rug and woollens for another. If the weight does vary slightly, compensate for this by cutting wider strips of the finer fabric.

Begin by making a small sample with your chosen materials to see if you like the thickness. To prepare braids for a coiled rug, cut rag strips of about 5cm (2in) wide and

Use this technique to create the Braided Woolly Rug on pages 42–44.

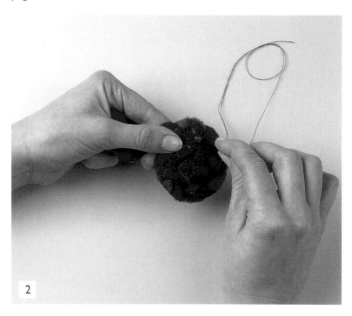

as long as possible. If the pieces are too short (under a metre) you will have to do a lot of stitching to join them together. Fasten the ends of three strips of fabric together with a safety pin and hook the pin over a cup hook screwed into something secure just above eye level. As you braid, fold the raw edges of the rag strips so that they are concealed within the folded strips. Start braiding near the pin by bringing the right-hand strip over the middle strip, then the left strip over the new middle strip. Continue braiding, turning the raw edges inside (1). When you are about to run out of rag strip, sew on a new strip and trim the seam to 0.5cm (¼in). Be sure to stagger these seams to avoid lumps in the braids. When you have finished, secure the loose ends with a pin.

To make a coiled rug, use a carpet needle and a heavy linen thread to sew first through the loop of one braid, then

through the loop lying beside it. Work backwards and forwards between the braids, coiling as you go and taking care that the braids remain flat and that the stitching is firm but not too tight (2). Continue until the rug is of the desired size.

To achieve a smooth finish on the edge of the rug, taper the last 25cm (10in) of each strip to about half the normal width. Finish the braiding and slip the tapered ends into the loop lying beside them. Secure in place, hiding the raw edges.

DESIGN YOUR OWN RUG

Once you have practised these techniques and gained in confidence, the next step is to design your own rug. You may get your ideas from textile collections in museums, paintings and drawings or from the many books that feature textiles and other decorative patterns. You may want to design a rug for a specific room and take your inspiration from this. Hooked, prodded and clipped rugs can be made in any shape; you could, for instance, design a rug to hug a piece of furniture such as a chair or to direct the flow of traffic around a room. Think about the existing colours and patterns in the room. You may want to use a motif from another fabric in the room, changing its scale to make a different impact.

Draw your idea on to paper the size of the rug you want to make and stand above it. Remember that the design will be viewed from different directions, so check it from all angles. Does the scale of the motif seem overpowering or too small? Is the rug the right size or does it seem to be lost among the furniture? You may want to trace the outlines of all the dominant shapes of the design on to a second piece of paper, then use them as templates to cut out rag shapes in the colours you are considering. Place these on top of the original drawing to get an idea of how the colour scheme and value balance looks within the room. Play around until you achieve a balance that pleases you.

FINISHING & CLEANING

Coating the back of a rug with a latex adhesive will prevent it from unravelling and make it firmer and less slippery. This can be done to rugs made with any rug technique, but is best for hooked, prodded and clipped rugs. Braided rugs benefit from being reversible and a latex backing prevents this.

Latex adhesive can be bought in hardware stores as a carpet-tile adhesive. Squeeze some on to the back of the rug and spread it around with an old credit card or a heavy piece of cardboard, pushing it into the gaps as you work. When you have finished coating the back of the entire rug with the latex adhesive (it will appear white before drying to a clear finish), you can fold down the hem of the rug and press it

into the latex. Leave to dry for 24 hours in a well-ventilated room. Cut the backing fabric to the same size as the finished rug plus 5cm (2in) all around for a hem. Press the hem under with a hot iron, then pin the backing over the reverse of the rug. Whip stitch the backing into place. Pin the twill tape over the hem seam and stitch into place. You may wish to apply another coat of latex adhesive to the back to prevent the rug from slipping on a wooden floor. See the individual projects for other ways to back rugs.

Clean the finished rag rug by vacuuming with a mild suction. If the rug becomes soiled, the best way to clean it is to dab the stain with a clean, damp cloth until the stain is gone. Never submerge the rug in water.

HOW TO USE THIS BOOK

The projects in this book have been chosen to both instruct the beginner and inspire the established rag-rug enthusiast. All of the projects are distinct and focus on a different area of rug making, whether it be use of colour, combining techniques, adding appliquéd elements or transferring a pictorial pattern onto hessian. Whilst the projects have not been formulated as a course to be strictly followed, the projects have been ordered from the simple through to the more complex and it is advisable that you complete some of the earlier projects if you are a beginner, before attempting the more ambitious designs.

You should have read through the introductory pages thoroughly as detailed descriptions of the basic techniques are not repeated in the projects. If you do begin work on a project and find there's something that you've forgotten or you need more information, refer back to these pages, you will find the answer.

Every project is clearly set out giving you all of the information that you need. A detailed 'you will need' list, step-by-step instructions with accompanying colour illustrations and full-colour photographs of the whole rug, as well as close-up details, bring the projects to life and make them easily achievable.

An at-a-glance 'specification' box gives you the size of the rug and the technique/s used, so you will automatically know whether the rug is the right size and has the right look for the room that you want to make a piece for. Examples of these elements are shown on this page.

Every rug has a helpful diagram and templates where appropriate. Because most of the rugs are simple or geometric in design, it shouldn't be necessary for you to enlarge the diagrams, they are there for you as a guide, they are not shown to a specific scale. Many have a grid already placed on them, or you can draw up a grid and place it over the diagram if it helps you. Instructions for the enlargement of templates have been given.

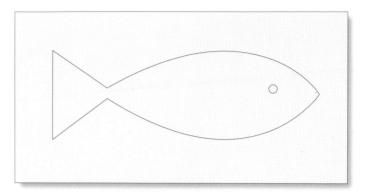

Template

Diagram

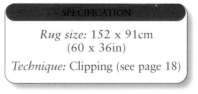

Specification box

Example of step-by-step illustration

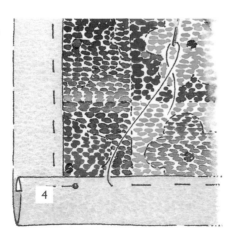

The satisfaction of making a rag rug is that there aren't any strict rules that have to be followed, you only need to know the basic techniques. Enjoy the creative freedom that this craft gives you.

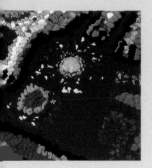

Projects
15 step-by-steps

Retro Flowers

Sara Worley

- Pencil
- Tracing paper
- Piece of card 20 x 20cm (8 x 8in)
- Cutting mat
- Craft knife
- Steel ruler
- 10-oz hessian 90 x 150cm (36 x 60in)
- Marker pen
- Frame
- Rug hook
- Selection of cotton and cotton/polyester fabrics cut into strips
- Dressmaker's pins
- Large-eyed needle and wool thread

SPECIFICATION

Rug size: 60 x 120cm
(24 x 48in)
Technique: Hooking
(see pages 15–16)

This very simple and cheerful hooked rug was inspired by the classic flower shape used in designs by Andy Warhol and Mary Quant in the 1960s. Four main colours of fabric were used, plus a touch of a dark colour for the centre of the flowers.

1 Enlarge the flower template by 190% and trace on to tracing paper. Transfer on to the piece of card, then place the card on the cutting mat and cut out with the craft knife.

2 Referring to the diagram on page 26, measure out and draw the grid on to the hessian with the marker pen (each square is 20cm/8in). Centre the flower template in each square and draw around it using the marker pen.

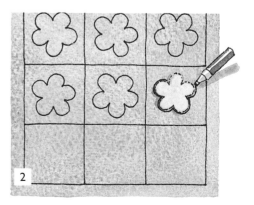

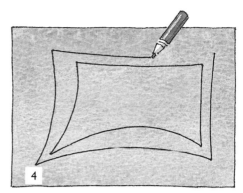

4

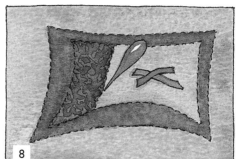

8

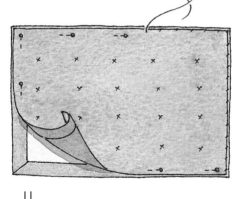

10

4 Referring to the diagram on page 27, draw the design on to the hessian. Attach the hessian to the frame, making sure that it is taut.

5 Using scissors or the rotary cutter and cutting mat, cut the dyed fabric into strips 1.5cm (½in) wide, then cut the strips into 9cm (3½in) clippings. Prepare a sizeable amount of fabric in each colour before you begin prodding.

6 Begin prodding on the right side of the hessian, which will form the back of the rug. Working on the outlines first, use the prodding tool to make a hole in the hessian.

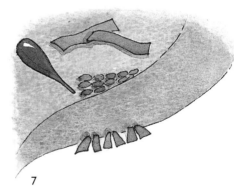

7

7 Push one of the strips of fabric halfway into the hessian with the prodder. Move along about three to four threads and make another hole. Push the other half of the fabric through with the prodder, using the fingers of one hand from behind the hessian to ensure that the ends are level. (The illustration shows what is happening on the right side and back of, the rug.)

8 Make another hole three to four threads away and repeat. Continue working in this way, completing the outlines, then filling in the rest of the hessian with blocks of colour until all the prodding has been completed. Remove the rug from the frame.

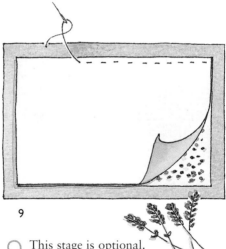

9

9 This stage is optional. Lay a piece of interfacing on the back of the rug with the adhesive side facing upwards. Sprinkle the dried lavender flowers evenly on to the interfacing, then lay the second piece of interfacing on top of the seeds with the adhesive side facing down. Press according to the manufacturer's instructions. Secure the interfacing to the rug with running stitches.

10 Apply latex adhesive along a 7.5cm (3in) border around the underside of the rug. Leave to dry for a few minutes, then fold over the 7.5cm (3in) border to the underside of the rug, pressing the hessian down firmly and cutting off the excess at the corners to achieve a neat, flat finish.

11

11 Lay the second piece of hessian over the back of the rug. Turning under a 7.5cm (3in) hem all the way around, pin the hessian to the rug. Hand sew the hem of the rug and the lining together with a strong thread in a matching colour. Make small cross-shaped stitches at intervals over the back of the rug, sewing through the layers to hold them in place.

12 On the right side of the rug, trim the pile to an even height with a pair of sharp scissors.

Amish no. 4
Nicky Hessenberg

You will need

- Rug canvas 73 x 75cm (28¾ x 29½in), 3 holes to 2.5cm (1in)
- Steel ruler
- Marker pen
- Wool blanket-type fabric in brown, blue, purple, green and red
- Rotary cutter
- Cutting mat
- Rug hook
- Scissors
- Blanket or newspaper
- Water spray
- Latex adhesive (optional)
- Lining material such as hessian, calico or a similar fabric, 80 x 80cm (31½ x 31½in)
- Dressmaker's pins
- Needle and strong sewing thread

SPECIFICATION

Rug size: 72 x 72cm (28 x 28in)
Technique: Hooking (see pages 15–16)

I have admired the designs and products of the Amish for some years. The simplicity of the clear, uncluttered lines, the geometric shapes and the colours used in the designs convey the impression of a serene and regular way of life. When looking through a book about Amish quilts, it occurred to me that many of the designs would transfer very successfully to hooked rag rugs. This is one of the designs I chose to adapt. I used two or three shades for each block of colour. This was purely a personal decision and not a design necessity for making the rug.

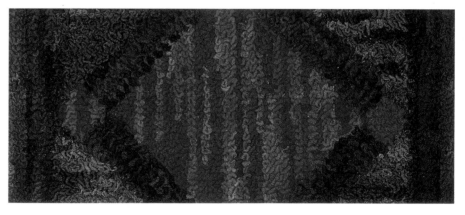

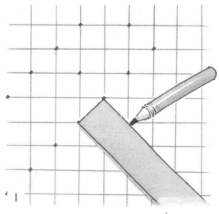

To neaten the rough edges at the top and bottom of the rug canvas, turn under a strip of three holes, making sure that the holes are in exactly the same place on both layers. Mark out the design on the rug canvas freehand, using the steel ruler and marker pen.

2 Cut the blanket fabric into strips about 1.5cm (¾in) wide, using the rotary cutter and cutting mat. Using the rug hook, pull a short strip of fabric through the canvas first to ensure that it is of the correct width to fill each hole in the canvas. If it is not wide enough, it will slip out of the holes; if it is too wide, the canvas will distort.

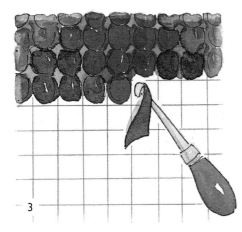

3

3 Using the rug hook, work the border first, starting in the middle of one side and working all the way around. Work along the rows, changing colour wherever this is indicated on the pattern. When a strip is finished, pull the end to the front of the rug and start working with a new strip. Insert it through the same hole as the end of the previous strip to ensure a firm fit.

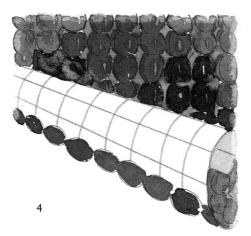

4

4 Check the underside of the canvas periodically to make sure that the loops are lying flat.

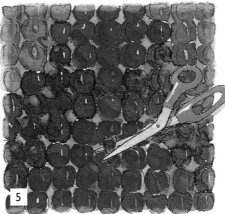

5

5 Once the pattern has been completed, trim the raw ends of the strips to the same height as the loops.

6 Place the rug on a blanket or some newspaper and spray with water to 'set' the loops. Leave to dry. If you wish to give the rug an extra-firm backing, apply a weak solution of latex adhesive to the back.

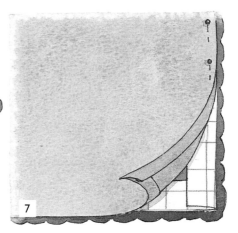

7

7 Turn under the two selvedges on the edges of the canvas. Lay the rug face down on a flat surface and lay the lining material on top of it. Turn the border under and pin the lining to the rug. Sew the backing to the rug with the strong thread.

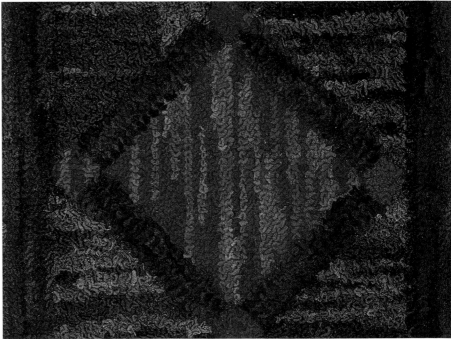

MAKER'S TIP

This rug is hooked with heavy wool blanket material that has been dyed and felted. Since the rag strips are so heavy, rug canvas has been used instead of hessian. The loft of the blanket wool holds the rags in place.

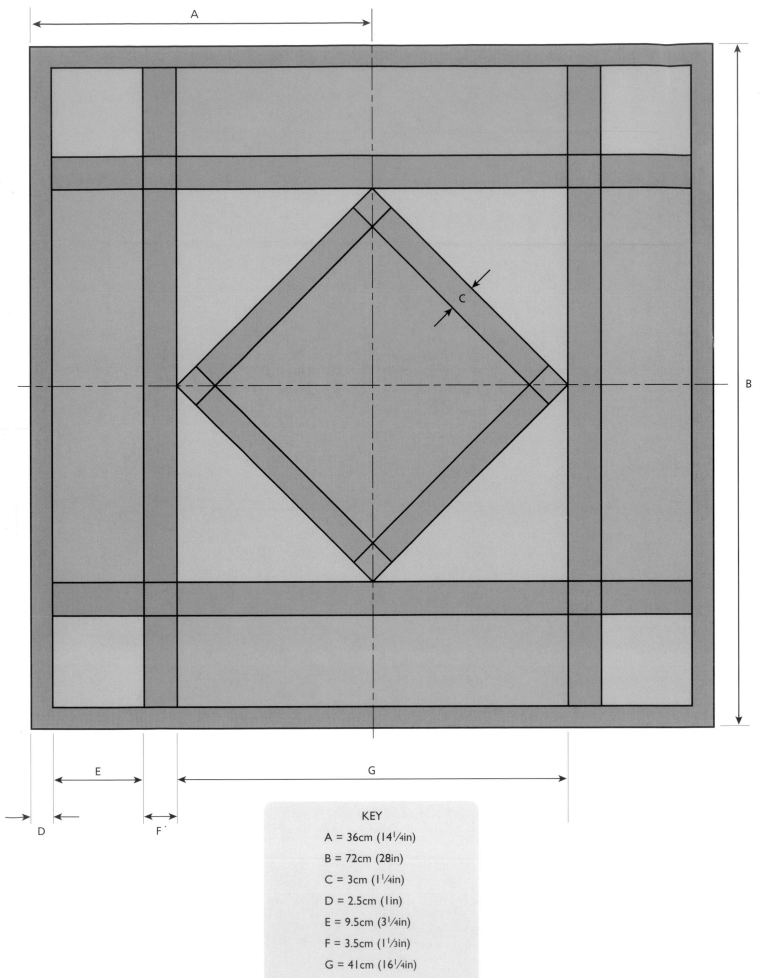

KEY

A = 36cm (14¼in)

B = 72cm (28in)

C = 3cm (1¼in)

D = 2.5cm (1in)

E = 9.5cm (3¼in)

F = 3.5cm (1⅓in)

G = 41cm (16¼in)

Cream Circle

Ann Davies
(Design by Piers Northam Interiors)

This rug is so effective because of its elegant simplicity. I was commissioned to make it for a private customer. It is actually a sampler piece for a much larger rug. The rug was to be placed in a bedroom in an apartment overlooking the River Thames and the designer, Piers, wanted subtle yet warm shades to complement the furnishings already installed.

You will need

- 12-oz hessian 100cm (40in) square
- Waterproof, black fine felt-tip pen
- Tape measure or steel ruler
- Scissors
- Medium-weight string
- Map pin
- Sharp, pointed HB pencil
- Frame
- Rotary cutter
- Cutting mat
- Cream silk noil 152 x 91cm (60 x 36in) wide
- Rug hook
- Cream wool flannel 200 x 183cm (80 x 72in) wide
- Prodding tool
- Cream carpet braiding 3cm (1¼in) wide, long enough to go around the circumference of the rug, with an extra 50cm (20in) to allow for shrinkage when washed
- Needle and strong cream thread
- Large towel
- Pressing cloth

1 Mark the centre of the hessian by folding it into four equal parts, then mark the centre with a dot, using the felt-tip pen. Place the hessian on a firm surface that will allow a pin to be pushed into it.

2 Measure and cut a piece of string 40cm (15¾in) long, plus an allowance for making a small knot at one end and a small loop at the other end to hold the felt-tip pen.

3 Make a small knot at one end of the string and a loop at the other. Push the felt-tip pen into the loop. Ensure that the pen is tightly held by the loop. Push the pin through the knot and pin it down into the hessian on the marked central point.

> **SPECIFICATION**
>
> *Rug size:* 80cm (32in) in diameter
> *Techniques:* Hooking (see pages 15–16), prodding (see page 17)

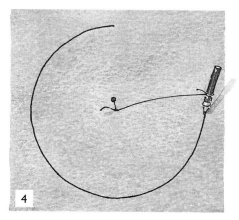
4

4 Use the string as a compass: keep it taut and move the pen around the hessian, marking out an 80cm (32in) circle. When this is done, remove the pin and string.

5 Refer to the diagram on page 37. With the pencil, mark out a grid of 15cm (6in) squares and 5cm (2in) wide bands on the hessian, measuring from the centre. Measure 7.5cm (3in) from the centre mark in each direction and mark out this square first. To draw lines on the hessian, drag the pencil down towards you through two threads of the hessian, exerting slight pressure on the pencil tip to ensure that it drags down through the hessian in a straight line.